The art book for children

Book two

Text by Amanda Renshaw

What's inside?

David Hockney

Who made the splash? Is he or she still in the water? Was it a beautiful, streamlined dive or a big bellyflop? Perhaps the person just jumped in.

What noise did the splash make?

Can you see anything else in the painting that might make a noise? The diving board might have squeaked when the diver jumped off, but everything else seems still and silent.

It looks like a very hot day, with no clouds, no breeze, and very little shade from the sun. No wonder the person chose to jump into the cool, refreshing water in the pool!

Although we recognize things in this painting—the house, the palm trees, the chair, the swimming pool—I don't think David Hockney wanted to make everything look lifelike. I think he wanted the sky, the water, the building, and the patio to look flat. It's almost as if this is not a painting of real things, but a painting of shapes:

Rectangles—
look at the windows,
the wall, and the patio.

Bands—
look at the shadow of the roof, the
blue edge of the swimming pool,
and the window frames.

Lines—
look at the trunks
of the palm trees,
the white line along
the edge of the pool,
and the lines of the
window frames.

A Bigger Splash

Spot the difference?

Here are four portraits of the same person. It's quite easy to tell which one was made first, but can you guess the sequence of the other three?

Self-Portrait at 28

Self-Portrait at 13

Here are some clues: in the second portrait the subject looks a little nervous, he is clean-shaven, and holds a plant. The next picture was painted after he had been on a journey that took him across snow-capped mountains. In the picture with the sitter at his oldest, he is facing directly toward us and not sitting at an angle.

All four pictures are self-portraits. Albrecht Dürer made the first when he was only 13, the second when he was 22, the third when he was 26, and the fourth when he was 28.

Do they all look like the same person to you? Dürer looks rather serious in all four pictures, and his lips look the same in each of them.

If you made a picture of yourself, how would you sit? There are so many choices to make. Where would you look? What would you do with your hands? What would the background look like? What would you wear—your favorite outfit, a hat, a scarf, or gloves?

Self-Portrait at 26

Self-Portrait at 22

	Age 13	Age 22	Age 26	Age 28
HOW IS ALBRECHT DÜRER SITTING?	at an angle	at an angle	at an angle	facing us
WHERE IS HE LOOKING?	to his left	at us	at us	at us
WHAT HAS HE GOT ON HIS HEAD?	a hat	a hat	a hat	nothing
WHAT'S HIS HAIR LIKE?	straight	straight	in ringlets	in ringlets
WHAT'S THE BACKGROUND LIKE?	plain	plain	a wall with a window	plain
WHAT'S HE DOING WITH HIS HANDS?	pointing	holding a plant	folded, wearing gloves	touching his fur collar
DOES HE HAVE A BEARD OR A MUSTACHE?	neither	neither	beard and mustache	beard and mustache
CAN YOU SEE HIS EARS?	no, both are covered	one showing	no, both are covered	no, both are covered

Dinner time

Casserole and Closed Mussels

Have you ever eaten mussels? They are a national dish in Belgium, where they are normally eaten with the most delicious fries.

But Marcel Broodthaers's mussels aren't for eating. First, the shells are all closed. If you are offered a bowl of mussels, you should only eat the open ones. The ones that are unopened will make you sick!

Also, these particular mussels wouldn't be very tasty—after all, they have been sitting in an art gallery for some time. They would be cold, and there may be some dust in the cracks between the shells. **YUK!**

But what's really wrong with this casserole dish full of mussels? Well, there are far too many mussels for the dish. But instead of overflowing and falling onto the table, they form a tall column. It's almost as if they are multiplying and pushing the lid up as they go.

Why did Broodthaers choose to make a casserole of mussels?
I think he is asking us to stretch our imaginations. Art doesn't have to be beautiful or special. Broodthaers is encouraging us to look at everyday things and wonder why they can't be art too. Broodthaers is from Belgium, so for him mussels are even more "everyday" than they would be if he were from another country.

(Wow! What a name! Broodthaers is difficult to pronounce. Just think of it in two parts: **BROOD-AIRS**. That's how his name should be said.)

A doodle

Do you ever doodle when you're bored? As you add more lines and shapes, do things sometimes emerge that are recognizable as animals, birds, or even people?

One day, Henry Moore was playing with a piece of wax, pushing and prodding at it with his fingers and thumbs until he thought it began to look like a strange head with horns, a beard, and a long thin nose. As he kept playing with it, the shape grew a crown and became, he thought, like the head of a king.

The fact that it looked more like a king's head to him than any other kind of head might have been because he'd recently been reading stories about kings, queens and princesses to his daughter Mary.

King and Queen

When he had finished the figure with the king-like head, Moore made a body and then added another person. *King and Queen* started life as a small piece of wax that you could hold in your hand and became a bronze sculpture that is 5 feet, 4 inches high. It now sits near the brow of a hill in Scotland looking south over a reservoir toward the English border. Have a look over the page.

Although this king and queen have no country to reign over, they do seem to command the beautiful landscape around them as they sit regally and serenely surveying their imaginary kingdom.

Moore made the king and queen appear regal by keeping the figures simple. Their feet are placed firmly on the ground in front of them. They sit comfortably, but don't slouch, and their hands, placed on their laps and on the bench, help them to appear calm and still.

Next time you start doodling, don't stop. Just imagine what it could turn into.

Henry Moore in his studio

King and Queen on Glenkiln Estate, Dumfriesshire, Scotland

A secret admirer

What kind of person do you think stands like this? One who is shy and awkward? Or one who is confident and sure of himself? Look at Thomas's clothes. He has a fur-lined cape draped over his arm, a plumed hat in his hand, and his silk suit is trimmed with lace. Even if you rented this outfit today for a costume party, it would be expensive. Can you imagine how much it must have cost in Thomas Coke's time, when there was no electricity, and there were no sewing machines, and everything had to be made by hand?

Thomas's clothes tell us that he was wealthy. The way he stands tells us he was confident. And I think that the way his dog sits quietly beside him, sniffing his hat and almost smiling, tells us that Thomas might also have been a kind person.

What else can this painting tell us about Thomas? The broken carvings in the lower right-hand corner do not mean he was a vandal who liked destroying buildings! They tell us he was interested in the art and architecture of ancient Rome. Thomas visited Rome several times, where he probably saw the sculpture of a woman that is behind him in this portrait. The sculpture was, and still is, in a famous museum that Thomas would most certainly have visited to see the Roman art that he loved so much.

Statue of Sleeping Ariadne

We can find out another thing about Thomas by looking at the portrait. Beneath his left hand there is some writing. It almost seems as if he is pointing to it. The words tell us that this picture was painted for a lady called the Countess of Albany. Although the Countess was married to someone else, it is said that she was in love with this handsome young man and that she asked Pompeo Batoni to make this lifesize portrait of him.

It is also said that the Countess looked very much like the famous sculpture of the sleeping woman. **Can you see the way the statue is looking toward Thomas?** Do you think the Countess might have asked Batoni to include this sculpture in the picture so that she could be with Thomas in the painting, even though she could not be in real life? Perhaps she also asked Batoni to make Thomas appear rich, confident, and kind because that's the sort of person she thought he was.

Thomas William Coke

Please touch the art

Surprising as it may seem, this pile of candies in brightly colored wrappers represents a person. The person it represents was called Ross. He was a close friend of the artist Felix Gonzalez-Torres and, sadly, Ross died when he was only a young man.

The pile of candies weighs 175 pounds, which is the same amount that Ross weighed before his death. However, this isn't the kind of portrait that's going to tell us much about Ross's character or what he looked like. Instead it's made to make us think about Ross.

When you are in an art gallery you usually need to be very careful not to touch the art that is on display. Gonzalez-Torres wants you to do quite the opposite. **Not only are you supposed to touch the pile, but you're also supposed to take a piece of it away.** And, of course, as people keep taking the candies away, Ross slowly disappears, just like he has done in real life. Taking a candy is like taking a piece of Ross away with you. It's a memento—something to remember him by.

What makes this "portrait" even more unusual is that after people have taken some of the candies away, more candies are added and the pile grows back. So, just as we can feel very sad when someone we know dies, our feelings can eventually grow back into happiness when we remember them.

Gonzalez-Torres must have loved Ross very much. It's as if he wanted other people to share Ross with him.

'Untitled' (Portrait of Ross in LA)

Happy couple

Today we take photographs to mark important events in our lives. There were no cameras in the middle of the eighteenth century (over 250 years ago) so, instead of photographers, painters were employed to paint pictures to remind people of happy occasions.

In November 1748, Frances Carter married Robert Andrews and they became Mr. and Mrs. Andrews. Rather than paint them on their wedding day, in a beautiful room, dressed in their formal clothes, as you might expect, Thomas Gainsborough has chosen to show the couple in the middle of the English countryside.

He did this for a very good reason.

Mr. and Mrs. Andrews

He wanted to tell us more than the fact that they had just got married.

He wanted to let us know that the wedding took place at the end of the fall—the sheaves of corn tell us this. He also wanted to tell us that the Andrews lived on a large estate in the country—just about all the land, as far as the eye can see, probably belonged to Mr. Andrews. Gainsborough could not have told us these things if he had painted the couple in a room.

Gainsborough may also have wanted to tell us that they were a relaxed couple, which would have been more difficult if they had been dressed in their wedding-day finery. Mrs. Andrews is sitting on an iron bench and Mr. Andrews is leaning on the arm of the bench with one leg crossed in front of the other. By painting him with a gun and dog I think that Gainsborough also wanted to tell us that Mr. Andrews enjoyed hunting.

Can you see that Gainsborough didn't finish this picture? Look at Mrs. Andrews's beautiful satin dress. There's an unpainted area on her lap. You can see the blank canvas. I wonder why the artist left it like this.

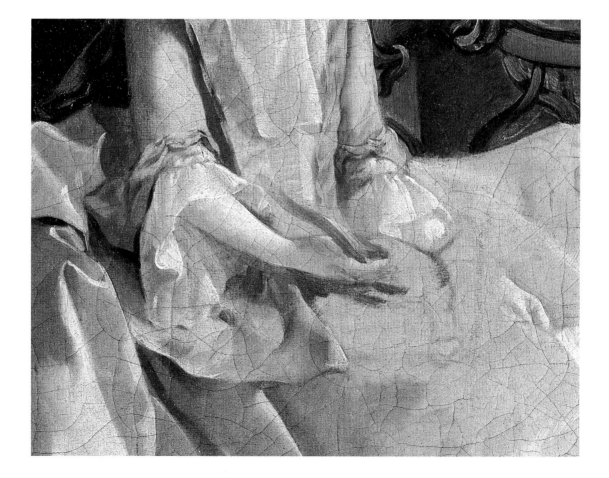

Was it for another dog or perhaps a bunch of flowers? Was he planning to add something at the last moment?

Never trust a painting!

René Magritte loved playing games and visual tricks.

The Betrayal of Images

Ceci … n'est … pas … une … pipe.

This … is … not … a … pipe.

Is this a French lesson gone wrong?

If it's not a pipe, what is it? Magritte is telling us not to trust what we see. Another painter might try to trick you into thinking that this is a pipe, but in fact it's not. It's a *painting* of a pipe.

If this man were really standing in front of a mirror like this, would we see the reflection of the back of his head or his face?

Is the landscape inside the room or outside the window?

The School of Athens

Classroom

Who are all these men standing in this vast hall?

This painting has become known as *The School of Athens*.

But what kind of school could this be?

Where are the desks?

Where is the teacher?

What is everyone chattering about?

Can you imagine the noise?

Does this remind you of your classroom?
I hope not! Look at some of the details on the following page.

There's a man lounging on the steps reading a piece of paper.

Another is writing something down as he leans against the wall.

A third man looks totally bored and is doodling without looking at what he is doing.

Somebody else is peering round another man's shoulder and copying what he's writing down.

These men are not paying attention because they are in fact all teachers rather than students. They are some of the greatest thinkers, mathematicians, scientists, geographers, artists, and inventors of all time, and, although they lived hundreds of years ago, their teachings are still used in schools today.

Raphael, the artist who made this painting (it's actually called a fresco because it was painted directly onto the wall), must have thought he was pretty special too, because he has included himself among these great teachers. You can find him on the far right. He is the second man in from the edge of the picture and he's looking straight at you.

It's easy to get carried away looking at all the different people in this fresco. But don't miss the absolutely enormous room they are standing in. Imagine its size! If you stood right next to the fresco, the men in the foreground would be about the same height as you. No wonder the fresco took Raphael over a year to finish.

The Construction Workers

Fernand Léger

Chutes and LADDERS

Six workmen are on a construction site. Four are carrying a heavy iron bar, another has just climbed a ladder and is standing above them, and the sixth sits even higher above him. This man seems to be holding on to another ladder.

What kind of building do you think this is going to be?

Will it be a low building or a tall one with many stories? The clue is in the background. You can see the deep-blue sky with white and gray clouds in it. This building is as high as the clouds, so it must be a skyscraper.

Look how Fernand Léger has included lots of ladders and ropes. The picture reminds me of a game of chutes and ladders. Maybe Léger was telling the construction workers to be careful not to fall!

Look at the way that he has painted the men. All but one wear a cap, but their shirts are all different and they all look as if they have really strong arms. Léger has painted the iron bars in bright, bold colors—red, yellow, black, and white. Imagine what construction sites would look like if the scaffolding, instead of being rusty brown and gray, was multicolored. Do you think the construction workers would prefer it?

Here are some real construction workers having a lunch break on scaffolding high above the streets of New York City.

Moving *fast* or standing **STILL?**

How fast do you think these boys are running? They look as if they are racing across the field as fast as their legs will carry them. You can almost hear their bare feet thumping on the grass. The boy with his blue jacket open is pulling the others as he charges across the meadow.

Snap the Whip

We know the boy is moving—but how does the artist make him look as if he's moving when, of course, a picture is totally still? Winslow Homer's solution was to include two opposites in the painting. He has included speed and stillness:

boys running ...

and boys standing completely still.

Just as you can feel that some of the boys are really running, you can also feel that the two boys on the right have really stopped. One boy is grabbing the other around his waist to ensure that he doesn't budge from his spot.

Have you ever played this game? It's called "snap the whip." In Homer's painting, a group of boys hold hands in a long line and run as fast as they can. Then, suddenly, without warning, the boys at one end of the line stop in their tracks. The others keep running and the rest of the line is yanked sideways. It's as if the line of boys is a whip that's been cracked or "snapped." You can see that the boys on the right have stopped and the boys at the other end of the line have been thrown off-balance and have fallen over because the jolt was so abrupt.

Have you noticed how most of the boys are barefooted, while the two who have fallen over are wearing shoes?

The lion tamer

A man in a long red cloak and hat sits at a desk reading a book. **I feel as if we shouldn't really be looking at him.** It's as if we are peering through a window into his private study; almost as if we are spying on him.

Everything appears calm and peaceful. A cat is curled up taking a nap and a lion is wandering around without a care in the world. The two birds in the foreground don't seem to be worried at all.

The man in the picture is Saint Jerome. As a young man he spent four years living in the desert, where he befriended a lion by removing a thorn from its paw. Later he became very famous for translating the Bible from Hebrew into Latin. Many, many artists have made pictures of him, but most of these paintings show him in the desert. **Why did Antonello da Messina choose to depict the famous translator instead of the man in the desert who saved a lion?**

Partridge

I think it's because Antonello himself was fascinated by facts. He had probably never seen a desert and didn't want to paint something where he had to rely on his imagination. Instead he has painted a room that looked like one he had actually seen and crammed it full of things that he knew. He tried to make the scene as lifelike as possible. The stone wall could almost be real. Look at all the different containers and books on the shelves. Can you see Saint Jerome's shoes at the bottom of the steps, another red hat lying on the bench behind him, the towel hanging from a hook, the curled-up note attached to the side of his desk, and the key? How about the partridge, peacock, and metal bowl on the ledge in the foreground and the columns and arches behind the lion? It is possible that Antonello had never seen a lion before, but he had to include him as a clue to tell us who this man is.

Next time you go to a museum, see how many paintings of Saint Jerome you can find without reading the label. Remember he might be in the desert and there will almost always be a lion and a red hat in the picture.

Saint Jerome in his Study

JUNK

Do you collect things? Comic books? Keyrings? Stickers? Shells?

This artist LOVED collecting things: coffeepots, shirts, toy cars, and clocks. He even collected trash from cans. When he had collected enough of one particular thing, he put them all together.

Arman's art isn't drawing, it isn't painting, and it isn't even sculpture. It's called "accumulation." To accumulate means to gather lots of things together. Arman gathered together many examples of the same thing, carefully attached them to each other, and called the things that he made "accumulations."

He stuck coffeepots together ...

Accumulation of Coffeepots

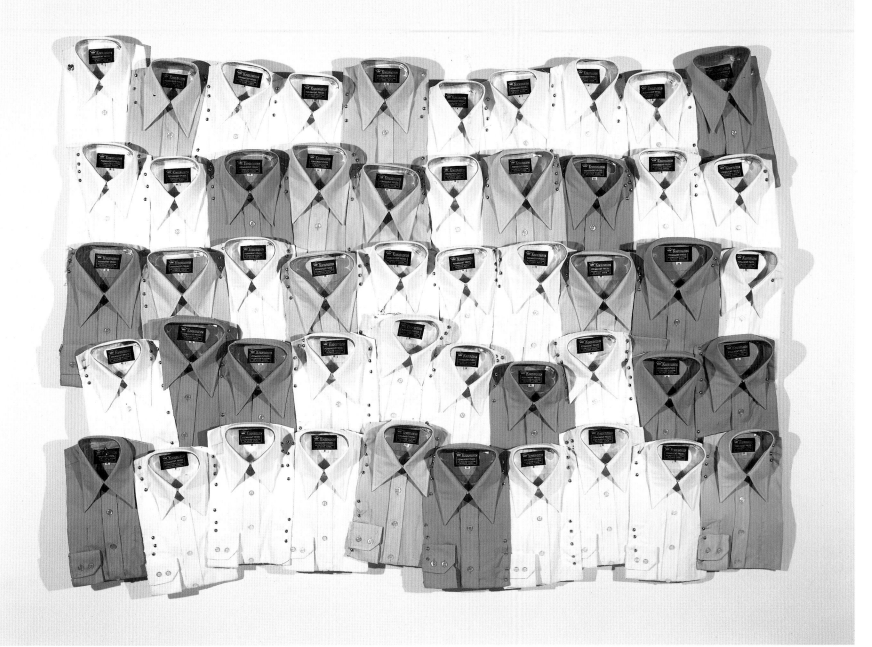

Permanent Press

and pinned shirts to a wall.

He put clocks in a transparent plastic case ...

O'Clock

and household trash in a glass box.

Household Trash in Glass Box

He collected toy cars, took them out of their boxes, and put them all in a case with a frame.

Matchbox

What could you do with your collections of things?

Arman's name was once Armand Fernandez. When he was on a hitchhiking vacation with friends, he decided that he wanted to be known by his first name only. So Armand Fernandez became known simply as Armand. Then, several years later, when Armand was about to have an exhibition of his work in a gallery in Paris, the printer who was making the catalog for the exhibition accidentally misspelled his name by leaving out the "d." Armand decided that, instead of correcting the mistake on the cover of the catalog, he would make the mistake correct by changing his own name. Armand became Arman.

Interior with a Girl at the Clavier

All calm

Look at the creases in this tablecloth. Someone must have ironed it very carefully. **Can you imagine taking it out of the cupboard, unfolding it, laying it on the table, and placing the three dishes on it?**

Can you also imagine what it would be like to stand in this room? It seems so calm and still. **Even the music being played would be gentle and relaxing;** definitely not loud and boisterous.

How does a painter make us feel this? The secret is to keep things simple. Look how simple this room is. Vilhelm Hammershøi has used very few colors and very few shapes. As far as the colors are concerned, except for a splash of yellow for the butter, he has really only used three.

| White | Dark brown | Lavender |

He has used the same shapes over and over again—squares and rectangles, circles and ovals. How many rectangles can you see? There are the two pictures on the wall. The wall itself is divided into two rectangles by its white decorative frame. There are also the rectangular shapes of the clavier (an old-fashioned kind of piano) and the lady's sheet of music. The rectangle of the table and the rectangles created by the creases in the tablecloth. How many circles and ovals can you see? There are the plates and the dish on the table, the glass lampshade and even the piano player's head is round. Hammershøi has repeated the same colors and shapes over and over again. I wonder if the pianist is practicing her scales and repeating the same sounds.

Is your home calm, with only a few shapes? Or is it busy with lots of different shapes, people, and loud music?

Messy mother

This is a party to celebrate the birth of a baby. The baby is wrapped in a red blanket and being carried by the man in a black hat.

However, most of the people here are women. The one on the right who is stirring something in a large saucepan seems to be the hostess. She must be the baby's mother. Let's hope she's more careful with the baby than she is with her cooking.

Look at the mess on the floor and all the broken egg shells!

Did you see Vilhelm Hammershøi's calm and restful room on the last page? Jan Steen's room is quite the opposite. It's noisy, boisterous, and messy. **Can you imagine yourself sitting on the red chair and watching everybody?** People are laughing, talking, and drinking. Can you imagine the sound of the ladies chattering, the mother calling out to ask if anyone wants more to eat, and the noise made by the lady pulling the red chair across the stone floor?

There is no simplicity and balance here. To make the scene appear busy and noisy, Steen has included lots of people doing different things. There are people facing us, people with their backs to us, people in profile, people moving and people sitting still. There are also lots of different shapes. See how many of these you can find: squares, circles, ovals, arches, rectangles, and triangles.

The Christening Feast

If you were going to paint an event taking place in your house, would you choose a quiet everyday moment, like Hammershøi, or a party? Which room would it be in?

Camembert clocks

The Persistence of Memory

What's your favorite kind of cheese? Do you prefer hard cheese like Cheddar, or soft cheese like Camembert? I don't know what kind Salvador Dalí preferred, but I do know that a ripe Camembert cheese helped him to paint one of his most famous paintings.

One evening, after dinner, Dalí felt very tired and had a headache. He decided to stay at home rather than go to the movies with his wife and friends. He had planned to go to bed early, but instead he sat for a long time at the dinner table, looking at the remains of the "super-soft" Camembert cheese they had eaten for supper.

Earlier that day, Dalí had been painting a picture in his studio. So far, he'd painted a beach and a rocky landscape by the sea with an olive tree that had most of its branches cut off. Otherwise the landscape was empty. After dinner and before going to bed, he went back to the studio and immediately knew what to fill the empty landscape with—clocks that looked like melting Camembert cheeses.

When his wife, Gala, came home from the movies, he made her close her eyes and sit down in front of the finished painting. "One, two, three, open your eyes!" he said. After she had looked at the painting for a while, Dalí asked her if she thought she would forget this painting in three years' time. "No," said Gala. "Once you've seen this image, you'll never forget it." I wonder if she was right. **Do you think you'll ever forget it now that you've seen it?** It's definitely very strange.

Dalí's paintings are quite unlike anybody else's. He was a rather unusual person too. He made extraordinary paintings, and he also did extraordinary things with his mustache!

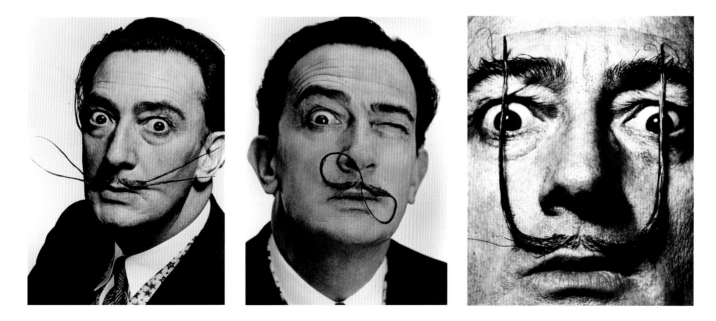

"January" from *Les Très Riches Heures du Duc de Berry*

Under the magnifying glass

The picture on the left is the size it actually is in real life. Look at all the tiny details. The artists must have used very delicate paintbrushes and a very large magnifying glass to make this painting. This picture and those on the following pages were all painted around 600 years ago to illustrate a book that was made for an extremely rich duke.

Printing presses had not been invented when this book was made, so all the pages were written and illustrated by hand. It might have taken many years to make a single book and, unlike today, each one was unique. Can you imagine holding and reading a book like this? **If it became your favorite you might think twice about lending it to somebody.**

This book was made by three brothers—Paul, Herman, and Jean (French for John) Limbourg. The paint they used was made from water, gum, precious stones, and plants.

 Some of the blues were made from a semi-precious stone called lapis lazuli,

 violet was made from sunflower seeds,

 green from the leaves of wild irises,

 and gold was made with real gold leaf.

Not only was this book unique, but it was very, very expensive to make.

Turn the page to see other pictures from this book. You may need your own magnifying glass to see all the details!

"January"

Can you see the duke's two little dogs wandering among the plates on the table?

"February"

Can you see the family sitting by the fire and the smoke rising from the chimney?

"March"

Can you see a shepherd and his dog watching over a flock of sheep?

"July"

Can you see the wooden footbridge leading to the triangular castle?

"August"

Two people are about to go into the lake and two others are already swimming.

"September"

Look at all the windows in the castle. What kind of person do you think lived here?

"April"

Can you see the spring flowers blooming in a walled garden?

"May"

Can you see the duke's two dogs playing around the horses' hooves?

"June"

On the right is the Sainte-Chapelle in Paris, a church that you can still visit today.

"October"

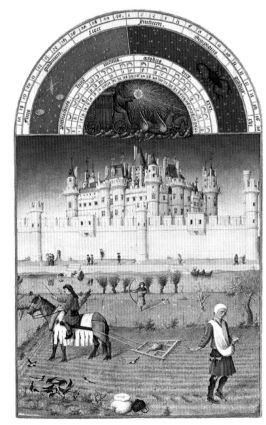

Can you see the scarecrow dressed like an archer?

"November"

The boars are greedily eating acorns that have fallen from the oak trees. Look how carefully the dog is watching them.

"December"

The duke was born in this castle on November 30, 1364. In which month were you born?

Wassily Kandinsky

Music to my eyes

Composition No. VII

Have you ever listened to music played by an orchestra, with violins, cellos, trumpets, clarinets, cymbals and drums? This painting is like that kind of music. I don't mean that it's a strange painting of people playing music. But if you could SEE music, it might look like this.

Can you imagine what this music might sound like? Would it be gentle and soothing or dramatic and loud with lots of different instruments playing, drums rolling and horns blowing?

I can imagine the long thin sound of a flute, the wobbly sound of an oboe, the whooshes made by violins, the warm swirling sounds of the cellos, the circular sounds of the trumpets, and the splash of the cymbals.

It takes an enormous amount of preparation to make a successful composition. A composer has to decide which instruments to use, which notes each one is going to play, for how long, and when. The painter has to decide the size of the canvas, which colors to use, what shape they will take, and where to put them.

Wassily Kandinsky spent many months planning this composition. He made hundreds of preparatory drawings, watercolors, and studies. Once the preparation was finished, he bought a canvas that was six-and-a-half feet high and ten feet wide and finished the painting in four days. At the end of each day, his wife took photographs to document its progress. These black and white photographs (color photographs didn't exist then) show us how Kandinsky made the picture.

November 26, 1913

November 27, 1913

November 28, 1913

November 29, 1913

He started towards the left of the canvas, painting the shape in the lower corner that looks a bit like a rowing boat, as well as the other single, dark colored lines. At the same time he painted some of the white background. Over the next three days he added the color and filled the canvas.

Kandinsky was one of the first artists to paint pictures that aren't of anything we can see or touch. He believed that an abstract composition of colors and shapes could be just as powerful and emotional as a painting of an amazing landscape, a battle scene, or even a piece of music.

What's your favorite piece of music? What would it look like if you painted it?

Cheating at cards

The Cheat with the Ace of Diamonds

The people around this table are all playing cards and, from the piles of coins on the table, we can see they are playing for money.

The man on the right with the beautiful embroidery on his collar, a red feather in his hat, and shiny, curly hair looks calmly at the cards in his hand.

The seated woman in the middle, who is wearing a brown dress and a pearl necklace, earrings and bracelets, looks as if she doesn't trust the woman standing next to her who wears a turban and avoids her gaze.

Whose turn is it?

The woman in the middle points toward the man on the left as if it's his turn.

The lady with the turban seems to be offering her a glass of wine. Maybe she's hoping that the drink will make her tipsy and stop her noticing that the man on the left is about to pull the ace of diamonds from the back of his belt!

Will the cheater be caught? Will the players rise to their feet in disgust, overturn the table, and send the cards and coins flying? Or, maybe, they'll calmly stand up and walk away? We'll never know.

There's a saying: "cheaters never prosper." Do you think this one will?

Crazy wallpaper

Have you ever decorated a room? Have you helped paint a wall or put up wallpaper? It looks as if Henri Matisse took a lot of red wallpaper printed with blue plants and flowers and laid it over the entire room, covering the table as well as the wall. The whole room seems to be moving with its swirling patterns of branches, flowers, and leaves. It even feels a little claustrophobic. Calmly standing on the right is a maid, carefully placing a bowl of fruit on the table. She is very still. Almost as still as the two glass bottles on the table.

Matisse was fascinated by the power of color. Some colors make us feel calm, while others are more exciting and busy. Red is definitely a busy color and with the swirling blues running through it in this painting, you can definitely feel the movement. By putting swirling patterns together with still objects, Matisse has created a picture that seems to be moving and still at the same time.

Not only did he love color, but Matisse also seemed to prefer curved lines to straight ones. Apart from the right angle of the window, the pink building in the distance and the chairs, this painting is filled with curvy lines and rounded shapes. Even the contours of the maid are rounded. Have you noticed how the shape of her hair is similar to the shape of the white blossom of the tall tree outside the window?

Color has a big effect on the space around you. If the walls of your classroom are white, the room will seem airy and spacious. But if they are painted deep red with blue swirling patterns, the room might feel as if it's moving. It might drive you a little crazy!

The Dinner Table (Harmony in Red)

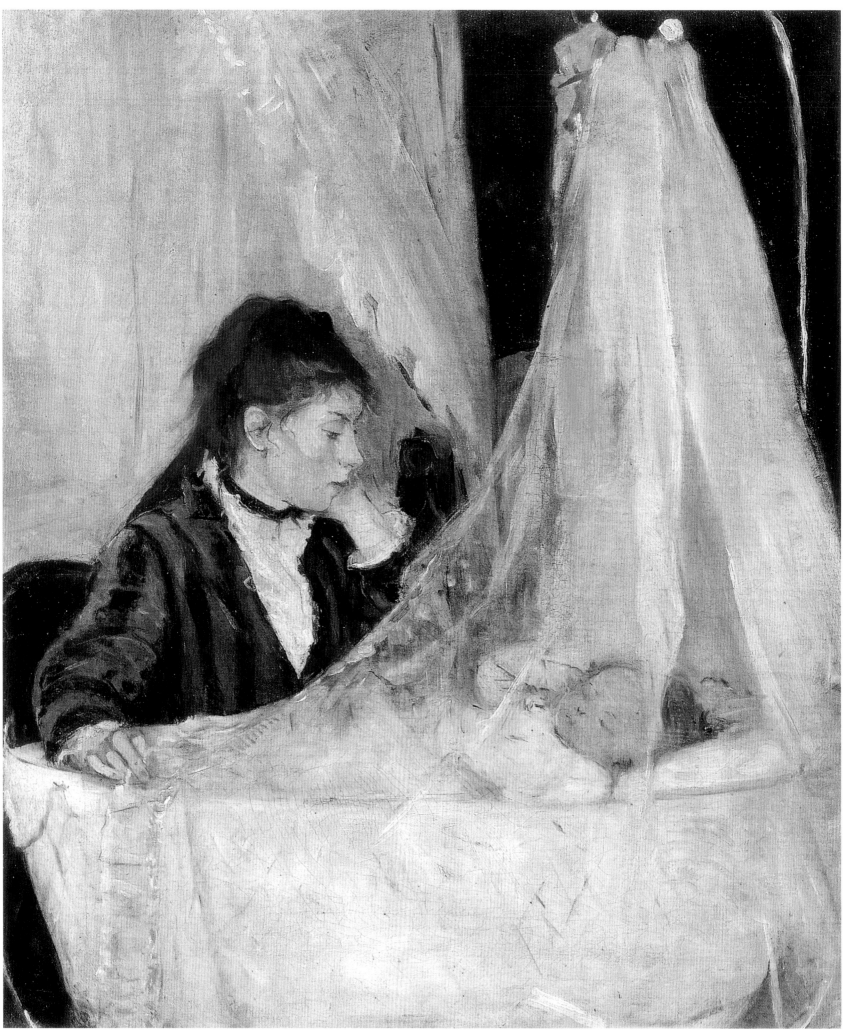

The Cradle

Mirror image

Do you know a baby as young as this one? Perhaps you have a tiny brother or sister yourself? If so, you'll know that babies sleep quite a lot and, when they do, you have to keep quiet around them.

This mother is watching tenderly as her baby sleeps. The atmosphere in the room is calm and quiet. I wonder how long she's been sitting there? We'll never know, but my guess is that she's been there for a while. She looks as if she is day dreaming. I like the way the artist has painted her absent mindedly playing with the fringe of the lace canopy with the fingers of her right hand. I wonder if she was doing this in real life, or if the painter chose to add this detail?

Look at how both mother and baby have one hand on their cheek and one arm bent at the elbow. They are like a mirror image of each other.

I also like the way the artist has managed to make the lace canopy appear transparent so that we can see through it. She must have painted the baby first and then very delicately added a thin layer of white and cream paint over the baby and crib.

The person who painted this picture was also a mother. She was one of a group of artists called the "Impressionists" who made many of their pictures outside in the open air. Berthe Morisot also painted outdoor scenes, but is best known for pictures of her own family. The mother in this painting is Morisot's sister, Edma, with her baby daughter Jeanne.

Winning the race

How quickly is this cyclist moving? Is he creeping along so slowly that his bicycle is wobbling? Or is he racing to win? Look at the way his shoulders are hunched and the way his hands grip the handlebars. Look at how the track beneath him seems to be whizzing by. I'd say he's cycling rather fast. We know he's in a race because we can see the grandstand behind him. We know he's not winning because there's another bicycle just ahead of him. You can see its back wheel on the left-hand side of the picture. I wonder if he'll be able to overtake the other cyclist and win.

We know that this race is taking place in France, because there is a French flag flying on the right-hand side of the painting. A sign beneath the flag reads, "*PNEUS*." This is French for tires. To the left of the cyclist there's another sign that's partly hidden by his chest. If you could see the whole thing it would read "PARIS-ROUBAIX." Even today, Paris-Roubaix is one of the toughest and most famous cycling races in the world. It is over 160 miles long and starts in Paris and ends in the town of Roubaix in Northern France.

Although for much of the race the cyclists have to ride over muddy cobblestones, the last stretch takes place in a large, outdoor velodrome (a cycling stadium) in the town of Roubaix. Our cyclist, in his green and black jersey, covered the same course over 90 years ago, as cyclists still do every year.

Jean Metzinger hasn't painted a very realistic scene. **The bicycle's wheels look as if they might collapse, and the cyclist is partly transparent—look at his face!** The painter's main aim was to show the sensation and tension of speed. Look at the whirring of the spokes on the wheel at the far left and look at the lines on the pavement that make the track appear to be zooming by. If you had to show speed in a picture how would you do it? Would it be like Metzinger or like Winslow Homer on page 28?

This is Charles Crupelandt, who won the Paris-Roubaix at about the same time that Metzinger painted his picture.

At the Race Track

Robert Campin and Assistant

The Merode Altarpiece

Breaking the code

This picture was probably made for the man and woman kneeling outside the door on the far left. It's likely that it hung in their home in Belgium. I wonder if their living room looked like the one in the picture.

Many experts and art historians have researched and written about this painting, but there are still unanswered questions about who actually painted it, who the people on the left are, and what the man on the right is doing?

It would take an entire book to try to get to the bottom of all the mysteries and we only have two pages, so let's focus on one thing. **Who is the man on the right and what is he doing?**

We know that the lady dressed in red in the living room is Mary. An angel has come to tell her that she is going to have a baby. According to the Bible, Mary's husband Joseph was a carpenter. That's who is in the right-hand picture. I wonder if he made the long wooden bench with the carved lions on its four corners and the strangely shaped dining table.

Scattered on the floor of Joseph's workshop and on his work bench are tools and other things we would find in any carpenter's studio: pieces of wood, a saw, an axe, a hammer, wood shavings, pliers, nails, and a screwdriver. Joseph seems to be drilling holes into a wooden board. I wonder if he's making another fireplace screen to protect Mary from the heat of the fire (it looks like a bit like the fireplace screen in the other room). But there's something else on the work bench that he made earlier. It's a mousetrap. There's a second one on the ledge outside the window. In the Bible, Joseph's role was to protect Mary. I wonder if the mousetrap is a kind of clue or a symbol—a way for the artist to tell us that Joseph created traps so that he could make sure that Mary and baby Jesus were safe.

Nothing is in this painting by chance. The artist has included lots of clues to help him tell the story: the lily in the vase, the snuffed-out candle, even the fact that Mary is sitting on the floor rather than on a chair. They all mean something. Artists often used to include symbols like these. Although, with some detective work, we can find out what they mean, the owners of the painting would have known straight away.

Glorious paint!

These two paintings are very different. It's easy to think that they might have been made by two different artists. In fact they were both made by the same person.

One painting is figurative. It represents something we can recognize. It's a portrait of the artist's daughter, Betty. Look at the detail. Gerhard Richter has concentrated on the red, white, and pink patterns of Betty's jacket and dress and the way in which her hair is gathered at the back of her head. The painting is so realistic that it almost looks like a photograph.

Betty

Abstract Painting

The other painting is abstract. It's not of anything we can see or touch. Richter has covered the entire canvas with thick paint and then dragged it across the surface with a squeegee. The result is a painting that, although it looks a bit like a graph showing the shock waves of an earthquake, is not supposed to look like anything we can recognize.

Many artists develop a way, or style, of painting that becomes their own and the more you see their work the easier it is to recognize it. Richter's work can be confusing because he paints in very different styles. Style is important to Richter, but the material with which he makes his art is even more important. There are many media to choose from: watercolor, stone, metal, paper, or pencil. Richter has chosen oil paint and canvas.

We can see that he is brilliant at making things appear very lifelike, but it doesn't matter to him whether they are lifelike or completely abstract. Richter just loves to explore different ways of using paint

What other ways of making pictures with this medium can you think of?

John William Waterhouse

Under a spell

This woman, dressed in white and drifting by in a strange boat, is called the Lady of Shalott. According to a legend she was cursed by a magic spell. She was imprisoned in a castle, forbidden to look out of the window, and only allowed to look at the world as it was reflected in a mirror. She never spoke, nor was she spoken to. She spent her days and nights at a loom weaving beautiful tapestries. **Can you imagine what it would be like, always alone and only able to see the world through a mirror?**

John William Waterhouse

The Lady of Shalott

One day the lonely Lady of Shalott saw the reflection of a handsome knight called Lancelot in her mirror. He was so good-looking that she could not help herself, and walked to the window to see him more clearly. As soon as she set eyes on Lancelot, her mirror shattered from top to bottom. Knowing that she had disobeyed the curse, she walked down the staircase of her tower, went to the river, found a boat, undid the chain that anchored it to the bank, climbed aboard, and let the boat drift down the river to the city of Camelot. As she drifted down the river, people heard her singing a ghostly song. These were the last words she was to utter. When she arrived at the castle of Camelot she was dead.

This story is told in a poem by the English poet, Alfred, Lord Tennyson. Even though it is only make-believe, Waterhouse's painting of it is so detailed that it almost looks like a photograph of an actual event in a real landscape. Look at the thick, embroidered tapestry, showing scenes of knights and castles, trailing in the water. This must have been something the Lady of Shalott had woven in the tower and brought with her on her last journey.

Even without knowing the story, you can tell there is something sad and gloomy about this painting. **How did Waterhouse manage to create this feeling?** I think it's something to do with the dark water and the dull, gray morning light. If he had painted the scene on a bright, sunny day, do you think we would feel the same sense of drama and tragedy?

Robert Mangold

Careful planning

Here's something for you to try. Pin an enormous piece of colored paper to a wall. Find a sharp pencil. Pull up a chair, ask a friend to hold it firmly, and climb on. Draw the largest oval you can manage. Reach as high as you can on your tip-toes and as low as you can by crouching down on the chair (but be careful not to fall off!). Make an oval that is so big you could walk through it.

This is about the size of the oval—or to be more precise, the ellipse, because it's longer and flatter than an oval—in Robert Mangold's painting.

Mangold plans his paintings very carefully. After several trials, he decides what shape each one will be, what color they will be painted, and exactly where the pencil lines will go.

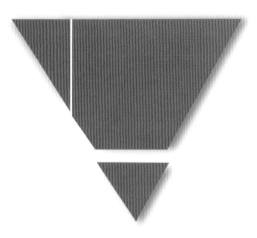

Paintings on canvas are normally rectangular; Mangold's hardly ever are. The painting on the right is a large triangle with the top sliced off and then turned upside down. Not only is it a different shape from most paintings, but it's also made up of two canvases. Can you see the join on the left-hand side? What color has he used? It's not really orange and it's not really brown. Mangold's colors don't come out of a tube. Instead they are carefully made by mixing several colors until he finds the perfect shade and tone.

Although his paintings are carefully planned, somehow they seem completely natural. His sweeping pencil lines are light and graceful.

Mangold works in a huge barn that he has made into a studio. Turn over the page and you can see him painting *Attic Series III.*

There are some differences between your drawing and Mangold's painting:

Mangold's painting is made on canvas, not paper.

You can see that Mangold started with the pencil line and then added the color.

As the title tells us, *Attic Series III* is the third painting in a series.

You can see *Attic Series I* (reddish brown) and *Attic Series II* (yellow) on the left-hand side of our picture.

Look at the paintbrush he uses. 👉

It's like one you might use to paint a wall, rather than a picture. This is so that he can achieve a very flat effect with the paint.

The other thing I didn't ask you to do was to take the chair and sit back to study your work like Mangold did.

Pictures of the past

The photographs on the opposite page were all taken by the same man in the same city. **Can you find the following things?**

—a man selling lampshades
—a ladies' underwear store
—the banister of a staircase
—an empty park
—a wall covered with posters
—an empty outdoor café
—a group of people watching an eclipse of the sun

The name of the photographer was Eugène Atget and the city was Paris. Atget took about 10,000 photographs of Paris. He wanted to take pictures of as many streets, houses, staircases, doorways, cafés, and stores as possible. If you put all his photographs together you could make an amazing collage of France's capital city.

Most people choose to take photographs of special events, buildings, or places. **Can you think of doing the opposite?** Instead of being careful about what pictures you take, photograph everything! Try walking down your street taking pictures of all the things that you don't normally notice: your front door, the car parked near the curb, people walking past, the intersection at the end of the road, or the plants that might be on the street. **Is anything growing in the cracks in the sidewalk?** What about the garbage in the gutter, or the entrance to your neighbor's home? Is their front door the same as yours?

When Atget was photographing Paris, he was always on the look-out for buildings or areas that were going to be destroyed. By photographing them his aim was to keep a record. Do you know of a building or a park near you that's about to be demolished? Perhaps you could be like Atget and photograph it so that in the future people will know what it looked like?

Rue Saint-Jacques

The Eclipse

Boulevard de Strasbourg

Tuileries

The Lampshade Seller

Le Dôme

91, rue de Turenne

ssshhhhhhhh

Why is the statue on the left of this picture telling us to be quiet?
Is he keeping a secret, or has he got something to hide?

There's another statue in the undergrowth. **Can you see it?** It is of two cupids playing with a large dolphin. Both cupids have wings and are sitting on the dolphin's back. Cupid was the Roman god of love and Jean-Honoré Fragonard has put this sculpture in the painting to tell us that love is in the air.

One of the two cupids is looking up at a girl dressed in a long, salmon-pink dress with lace trim. She's on a swing that's hanging from the branch of an old oak tree. The girl is wearing a summer hat, and a creamy-pink ribbon is tied in a bow around her neck. The frills on her cuffs and around the hem of her skirt and petticoats are similar to the patterns made by the branches and leaves above her.

This is a playful picture. I don't think it's meant to be serious, or even realistic! A swing would never swing in a straight line if it was tied to a branch like this. And if anybody ever sat on this swing I'm sure they would slip right off the back!

Behind the girl is a man in a powdered wig and a blue suit. He is pulling on two ropes, making the swing go higher. But the girl's not taking any notice of him. Instead, she's waving at another man, also in a powdered wig and blue suit, who is hiding in the bushes beneath her. In fact, she's just flicked off her dainty satin slipper for him to catch. **I wonder if he'll catch it or miss it, because he seems to be looking up her skirt!**

The beautiful girl on the swing appears to have two men competing for her attention. The man pulling on the ropes is older and more serious—he's not smiling much. The man hiding in the bushes is younger and perhaps a bit more playful. The statue with his finger to his lips is telling us to be quiet. Sssssshhhh—don't let the older man know that the younger one is there!

The Swing

Cake cartoons

Cartoons exaggerate people's features—they make their ears bigger, their noses longer, their eyes closer together, their eyebrows thicker, or their hair colour lighter if it's blonde, and darker if it's brown.

Mickey Mouse is a cartoon of that little gray animal that squeaks and eats cheese. He doesn't look like a real mouse. His ears are too big and his nose is too round, but we still know that he is a mouse.

If I asked most people to think of a cartoon of a piece of cake they'd think I was rather strange—until they had seen a painting by Wayne Thiebaud. Thiebaud's cakes—chocolate cakes, cakes with green frosting, cakes with strawberries on top, and cheesecakes—are like cartoons.

They don't look like real cakes, but there's no mistaking them for what they are. They look tastier, sweeter, and most deliciously messy to eat. The one with the pale green frosting would be very difficult to eat without getting it all over your face. **Can you imagine what they would taste like?** My favorite would be one of the chocolate cakes in the front row. Which one would you choose?

Of course, cartoons are also supposed to be fun and make you smile. You can't say that these cakes look serious. In fact they look like fun cakes to me. How would you draw a cartoon of a thing rather than a person? When you start thinking about it you realize how difficult it is.

Various Cakes

Spts

The painting on the following pages is all about spots. **There are plenty of things for you to spot:**

Can you spot a boat that looks like it is sinking?

Can you spot a girl with a small bunch of flowers?

Can you spot a lady fishing?

Can you spot a man playing a trombone?

Can you spot a little girl dressed in white?

There are eight parasols, seven open and one closed. Can you spot them all?

Can you spot a lady taking a monkey for a walk?

In addition to the things you can spot, the painting itself is actually made up of spots—thousands of tiny spots, or dabs, of paint. Georges Seurat said that he made this and other paintings with "points" of paint. So his style of painting was called "pointillism."

Most painters who lived at the same time as Seurat mixed their paints on a palette. Seurat did not. He used a small brush to put tiny dots of each color directly from the paint tube onto the canvas. He discovered that if you put dots of different colors close to one another and stand back from the painting, your eyes make the colors blend. Close up you see lots of tiny dots of different colors. From a distance you can see people taking a stroll on a Sunday afternoon—have a look over the page.

Lifesize detail of *A Sunday on la Grande Jatte*

Seurat liked the dots so much that he covered the picture frame with them too!

A Sunday on la Grande Jatte

Want to know more?

Antonello da Messina Page 31
Saint Jerome in his Study, about 1475
oil on wood panel
18 x 14 1/2 in (45.7 x 36.2 cm)
National Gallery, London, England

Antonello da Messina takes
his name from his birthplace,
Messina on the Italian island
of Sicily. He was born between
1429 and 1431, and he died
there in 1479.

Arman Page 32
Accumulation of Coffeepots, 1962
welded metal coffeepots
20 1/2 x 17 1/4 x 19 in (52 x 44 x 48 cm)
Private collection

Page 33
Permanent Press, 1977
accumulation of shirts
50 x 63 3/4 in (127 x 162 cm)
Private collection

Page 34 (from left to right)
O'Clock, 1998
alarm clocks in a Plexiglas box
47 1/4 x 35 1/2 x 6 3/4 in
(120 x 90 x 17 cm)
Private collection

Household Trash in Glass Box, 1959
debris in glass box
26 x 16 x 3 in (65.5 x 40 x 8 cm)
Private collection

Page 35
Matchbox, 1964
toy cars and boxes in a Plexiglas box
14 x 25 x 2 3/4 in (35.5 x 63.5 x 5.5 cm)
Private collection

Arman (whose real name was
Armand Fernandez) was born
in Nice, France, in 1928. As well
as being an artist, he was also
a Judo teacher. He died in
2005 in New York City, USA.

Atget Page 67 (top row)
Rue Saint-Jacques, 1899
black-and-white photograph

The Eclipse, 1912
black-and-white photograph

(middle row) *Boulevard de Strasbourg*, 1912
black-and-white photograph

Tuileries, 1912
black-and-white photograph

The Lampshade Seller, 1899
black-and-white photograph

(bottom row) *Le Dôme*, 1925
black-and-white photograph

91, rue de Turenne, 1911
black-and-white photograph

Eugène Atget was born in
Libourne, France, in 1857.
He lived in Paris during the
1890s and died there in 1927.
It is said that after the age
of 50, Atget ate nothing
but bread, milk, and sugar!

Batoni Page 14
Statue of Sleeping Ariadne,
AD 130–40
Vatican Museums, Rome, Italy

Page 15
Thomas William Coke, 1774
oil on canvas
96 3/4 x 67 in (245.8 x 170.3 cm)
Holkham Hall, Norfolk, England

Pompeo Batoni was born in
Lucca, Italy, in 1708, where he
taught himself to paint. He
died in Rome, Italy, in 1787.

Broodthaers Page 8
Casserole and Closed Mussels, 1964
mussel shells, polyester, and
iron casserole dish
12 in (30.5 cm) high
Tate, London, England

Marcel Broodthaers was born
in Brussels, Belgium, in 1924.
He died in Cologne, Germany,
on his 52nd birthday in 1976.

Campin and Assistant
Pages 56–7
The Merode Altarpiece, 1425–30
oil on wood
central panel 25 1/4 x 25 in
(64.1 x 63.2 cm), each wing 25 1/4 x 10 3/4 in
(64.5 x 27.3 cm)
Metropolitan Museum of Art,
New York, USA

Not a lot is known about
Robert Campin, but we think
he was born around 1380 in
Tournai, Belgium, and he was
certainly making paintings
by 1406. He died in 1444
in Tournai.

Dalí Page 40
The Persistence of Memory, 1931
oil on canvas
9 1/2 x 13 in (23 x 34 cm)
Museum of Modern Art,
New York, USA

Page 41
Three black-and-white photographs
of Dalí's mustache taken by Philippe
Halsman in 1954

Salvador Dalí was born in
Figueres, Spain, in 1904, and
he died there in 1989. During
his career, Dalí produced over
1,500 paintings.

Dürer Page 6 (left to right)
Self-Portrait at 28, 1500
oil on panel
26$\frac{1}{2}$ x 19$\frac{1}{4}$ in (67 x 49 cm)
Alte Pinakothek, Munich, Germany

Self-Portrait at 13, 1484
silverpoint on paper
11 x 7$\frac{3}{4}$ in (28 x 20 cm)
Albertina, Vienna, Austria

Page 7 (left to right)
Self-Portrait at 26, 1498
oil on panel
20$\frac{1}{2}$ x 16$\frac{1}{4}$ in (52 x 41 cm)
Prado Museum, Madrid, Spain

Self-Portrait at 22, 1493
oil on parchment on canvas
22$\frac{1}{2}$ x 17$\frac{3}{4}$ in (57 x 45 cm)
Louvre Museum, Paris, France

Albrecht Dürer was born in 1471 in Nuremberg, Germany (one of 18 children!), and he died there in 1528.

Fragonard Page 69
The Swing, 1767
oil on canvas
32 x 25$\frac{1}{2}$ in (81 x 64.2 cm)
Wallace Collection, London, England

Jean-Honoré Fragonard was born in Grasse, France, in 1732. He died in Paris, France, in 1806.

Gainsborough Page 18
Mr. and Mrs. Andrews, 1750
oil on canvas
24$\frac{1}{2}$ x 47 in (69.8 x 119.4 cm)
National Gallery, London, England

Thomas Gainsborough was born in the English village of Sudbury in Suffolk, in 1727. He died in London, England, in 1788.

Gonzalez-Torres Page 17
'Untitled' (Portrait of Ross in LA), 1991
candies, individually wrapped in multicolored cellophane
variable dimensions
Art Institute of Chicago, Illinois, USA

Felix Gonzalez-Torres was born in Guáimaro, Cuba, in 1957. He moved to New York City, USA, in 1980, and died there in 1996.

Hammershøi Page 36
Interior with a Girl at the Clavier, 1901
oil on canvas
22 x 17 in (56 x 44 cm)
Private collection

Vilhelm Hammershøi was born in Copenhagen, Denmark, in 1864. He did most of his work in his native city, where he died in 1916. In 1997 one of his paintings was used on a Danish postage stamp.

Hockney Page 5
A Bigger Splash, 1967
acrylic on canvas
96 x 96 in (243.8 x 243.8 cm)
Tate, London, England

David Hockney was born in 1937 in Bradford, England. He now lives and works in California, USA.

Homer Page 28
Snap the Whip, 1872
oil on canvas
22 x 36 in (55.9 x 91.4 cm)
Butler Institute of American Art, Youngstown, Ohio, USA

Winslow Homer was born in 1836 in Boston, Massachusetts, USA. He died in Prout's Neck, Maine, USA, in 1910.

Kandinsky Page 46
Composition No. VII, 1913
oil on canvas
78$\frac{3}{4}$ x 118 in (200 x 300 cm)
State Tretyakov Gallery,
Moscow, Russia

Page 47
Four black-and-white photographs of *Composition No. VII* in progress taken by Grabriele Münter in 1913

Wassily Kandinsky was born in 1866 in Moscow, Russia. He died in Paris, France, in 1944.

La Tour Page 48
The Cheat with the Ace of Diamonds, 1635
oil on canvas
41$\frac{3}{4}$ x 57$\frac{1}{2}$ in (106 x 146 cm)
Louvre Museum, Paris, France

Georges de La Tour was born in Vic-sur-Seille, France, in 1593 and died in Lunéville, France, in 1652. During his career he produced works for King Louis XIV of France.

Léger Page 26
The Construction Workers, 1950
oil on canvas
118 x 78$\frac{3}{4}$ in (299.8 x 200 cm)
Fernand Léger Museum, Biot, France

Page 27
Charles C Ebbets
Lunch on a Skyscraper, 1932
black-and-white photograph

Fernand Léger was born in Argentan, France, in 1881. He lived in the USA during World War II, but later returned to France where he died in Gif-sur-Yvette, France, in 1955.

Limbourg Brothers
Pages 42, 44–5
Pages from *Les Très Riches Heures*
du Duc de Berry, 1412–16
ink on vellum
9 x 5¹/₂ in (22.5 x 13.6 cm)
Condé Museum, Chantilly, France

The Limbourg brothers, Paul,
Herman and Jean, were born
in Nijmegen, the Netherlands,
in the 1380s. They all died
of unknown causes, probably
of the plague, in 1416.

Magritte   Page 20
The Betrayal of Images, 1928–9
oil on canvas
25³/₈ x 37 in (64.5 x 94 cm)
Los Angeles County Museum of Art,
California, USA

Page 21 (left to right)
The Human Condition, 1933
oil on canvas
39¹/₂ x 32 in (100 x 81 cm)
National Gallery of Art,
Washington, DC, USA

Not To Be Reproduced, 1937
oil on canvas
32 x 25¹/₂ in (81 x 65 cm)
Private collection

René Magritte was born in
Lessines, Belgium, in 1898.
As a young man he worked
in a wallpaper factory.
Magritte died in 1967 in
Brussels, Belgium.

Mangold   Page 63
Attic Series III, 1990
acrylic and colored pencil on canvas
90¹/₈ x 122 in (229 x 310 cm)
Private collection

Pages 64–5
The artist at work in his studio, 1990
color photographs

Robert Mangold was born in
North Tonawanda, New York,
USA, in 1937. He currently
lives in Washingtonville,
New York, USA.

Matisse   Page 51
The Dinner Table (Harmony in Red), 1908
oil on canvas
71 x 86¹/₂ in (180 x 220 cm)
Hermitage Museum, St Petersburg, Russia

Henri Matisse was born in
Le Cateau-Cambrésis, France,
in 1869. He moved to the
French Riviera in 1917, where
he remained for the rest
of his life. He died in Nice,
France, in 1954.

Metzinger   Page 54
Charles Crupelandt, about 1912
black-and-white photograph

Page 55
At the Race Track, about 1914
oil and collage on canvas
51³/₈ x 38³/₈ in (130.4 x 97.1 cm)
Peggy Guggenheim Collection,
Venice, Italy

Jean Metzinger was born in
Nantes, France, in 1883. After
serving in World War I, he
moved to Paris, France, where
he lived until his death in 1956.

Moore   Pages 10, 12–13
King and Queen, 1952–3
bronze
64 in (164 cm) high
Glenkiln Estate, Dumfriesshire, Scotland

Page 11
Henry Moore in Hoglands Maquette
Studio, Perry Green, 1963

Henry Moore was born
in Castleford, West Yorkshire,
England, in 1898. He died in
1986 in Much Hadham,
Hertfordshire, England.

Morisot   Page 52
The Cradle, 1872
oil on canvas
22 x 18 in (56 x 46 cm)
Musée d'Orsay, Paris, France

Berthe Morisot was born in
Bourges, France, in 1841. She
married Eugène Manet
(brother of the artist Edouard
Manet) in 1874, and lived in
Paris, France, until her death
in 1895.

Raphael   Pages 22–3
The School of Athens, 1508–11
fresco, 303 in (770 cm) width at base
Vatican Museums, Rome, Italy

Raphael Santi was born in the
town of Urbino, Italy, in 1483.
He was one of the greatest
painters of the Renaissance
and one of the favorite
artists of Pope Julius II. He
died in Rome, Italy, in 1520.

Richter Page 58
Betty, 1988
oil on canvas
$40^{1}/_{8}$ x $28^{3}/_{4}$ in (102 x 72 cm)
St Louis Art Museum, Missouri, USA

Page 59
Abstract Painting (no. 794–1), 1993
oil on canvas
$94^{1}/_{2}$ x $94^{1}/_{2}$ in (240 x 240 cm)
Private collection

Gerhard Richter was born in
Dresden, Germany, in 1932. In
1961 he moved from what was
formerly East Germany to
Düsseldorf in West Germany,
and from 1983 he has lived
in Cologne, Germany.

Seurat Pages 74–5
A Sunday on la Grande Jatte, 1884–6
oil on canvas
$81^{3}/_{4}$ x $121^{1}/_{4}$ in (207.5 x 308 cm)
Art Institute of Chicago, Illinois, USA

Georges-Pierre Seurat was
born in Paris, France, in 1859. It
took Seurat two years to paint
all the dots in the picture on
pages 74–5. He died in Paris at
the age of 31 in 1891.

Steen Page 39
The Christening Feast, 1664
oil on canvas
35 x $42^{3}/_{4}$ in (89 x 109 cm)
Wallace Collection, London, England

Jan Steen was born in Leiden,
the Netherlands, in about
1626. After living in various
parts of the country, he
returned to Leiden in 1669
and died there in 1679.

Thiebaud Page 71
Various Cakes, 1981
oil on canvas
25 x 23 in (63.5 x 58.4 cm)
Private collection

Wayne Thiebaud was born
in the American town of Mesa,
Arizona, in 1920. One of
his first jobs was drawing
a comic strip for the Walt
Disney Studios.

Waterhouse Page 60
The Lady of Shalott, 1888
oil on canvas
$60^{1}/_{2}$ x $78^{3}/_{4}$ in (153 x 200 cm)
Tate, London, England

John William Waterhouse was
born in Rome, Italy, in 1849,
and moved to England a year
later. He died in 1917 in
London, England.

Picture Credits

Phaidon Press Inc.
180 Varick Street
New York
NY 10014

www.phaidon.com

First published 2007
© 2007 Phaidon Press Limited

ISBN 978 0 7148 4706 1 (US Edition)

Concept design by Alan Fletcher, designed by Lucy Newell
Printed in China

If you have enjoyed this book, why not read
The Art Book for Children Book One:

ISBN: 978 0 7148 4706 1